Look at the Child

an expression of Maria Montessori's insights

by
Aline D. Wolf

"Only the child himself can teach us to know him."
— Montessori

Principal Photographer — Don Baker

Contributing Photographer — John Rudasill

Calligrapher -- Dana Detwiler

My special thanks to
Eugenia Bagley, Paula Benjamin and Marilyn Goldberg
for editorial assistance.

Library of Congress Catalog Card Number 78-58153
International Standard Book Number 0-9601016-2-4

Books-Posters-Slides

P.O. Box 767
Altoona, Pennsylvania 16603

Introduction

When Maria Montessori was 81 years old, a special event was held to honor this woman who had spent almost fifty years working for the rights of the young child. She was honored by dignitaries, educators and children from seventeen countries who gathered in London for the 1951 International Montessori Congress. After listening to many compliments for her educational work which had reached every continent, Maria Montessori addressed the crowd with a vitality that was amazing for her age. Scolding her admirers, she implied that their tributes had missed the point. They focused on Maria Montessori, the woman, rather than on the subject of her life's work. *"I am but a finger pointing to something beyond myself,"* she told them. *"Look not at the outstretched finger but at what it is pointing to. Look at the child."*

In the years when Maria Montessori began her work, first as a physician and then as an educational innovator, children were most often regarded as little adults. Their progress and behavior were not judged according to their own laws of development but according to the adult standards of the day. No special attention was given to children's mental capacities until they were six or seven years old. Then they began school in a rigid classroom where their speech and movement were curtailed and their natural curiosity and initiative were ignored. Children were expected to learn what adults decided to teach them.

It was Maria Montessori's particular genius to see the child as he really was, not as a little adult, but as a unique species whose work was *"to create the man he will become."* She has taught us to recognize that all his energies are fixed by nature on this task, and his choice of activities is guided by an inner voice which constantly directs him to those exercises which serve the immediate phase of his development. A young child, for example, may climb the stairs twenty times a day, not because he has to get to the second floor, but because the act of climbing is, at that point, essential to his maturation.

When allowed to follow his individual interests, a child is guided by a simple and delightful intelligence; he has a way of learning that is entirely different from that of an adult. By continually observing, hearing, feeling, lifting, pushing, pulling, opening, closing, climbing, smelling, licking and dropping the things in his everyday world, a child can assimilate all kinds of information without any conscious or tedious effort to do so. Referring to this intelligence as an *"absorbent mind,"* Montessori tells us, *"The child learns everything without knowing he is learning it, treading always in the path of joy."* When a parent or teacher recognizes and cultivates this natural process of learning, then a child's education is not only productive — it is in harmony with life itself.

When Montessori asks us to *"look at the child,"* she wants us to do more than simply glance or admire. She asks us to watch carefully as the child, through his everyday activities, reveals his nature to us. *"The child has his own laws of development; it is a question of following these, not of imposing ourselves upon him."* If we understand the inner forces at work in his life, we can then arrange an environment that will be appropriate for his natural urges to explore.

The adult, especially a parent, is usually the most significant single influence in this environment and, as such, can enhance or can actually retard the child's development. The grown-up is almost always well intentioned, but not always well informed. On this point Montessori warns us, *"Unless we adults are enlightened as to the way his mind develops, we are likely to become the greatest obstacle to his progress."*

"The adult environment," Montessori tells us, *"is not a life-giving environment for the child."* Deviations in a child's behavior may begin as early as his first experience in an adult atmosphere where he encounters a fragile or potentially dangerous object. The command "Don't touch" which the child then hears from an adult is a direct contradiction to his strong natural urge to handle everything in sight. It is almost impossible for the toddler to suppress his own desire and follow the adult's wishes. *"Before the child is three, he cannot obey unless the command he receives corresponds with one of his vital urges. He may succeed in obeying an order once, but he cannot do it next time. It is a period in which obedience and disobedience seem to be combined."*

Montessori believed that the child could develop self-discipline when he was given some freedom in an appropriate environment. This did not mean allowing the child to act irresponsibly without any kind of restraint. It meant offering the child a choice of activities, allowing him freedom to exercise his movements, to examine things with all his senses, to follow his own pace, to repeat an activity as many times as he chose and to be free from interruptions whenever he was concentrating.

In Montessori's view, freedom did not signify chaos. She recognized that *"the need for order is one of the most powerful incentives to dominate a child's early life."* She continually urged adults to take advantage of the very young child's sensitive period for order by giving him child-size furniture and utensils and assigning a particular place for each of his possessions. The child could then take delight in maintaining order in his own small area of responsibility.

This kind of work helps the child to develop character far more effectively than lectures from an adult. *"The commonest prejudice in ordinary education,"* Montessori writes, *"is that everything can be accom-*

plished by talking or by holding one's self up as a model to be imitated, while the truth is that the personality can only develop by making use of its own powers."

Montessori did not direct her words to any one group of parents or teachers. During her long lifetime, she observed children on every continent. *"My experience of over forty years,"* she wrote, *"with children of all races, of different religions, belonging to the most divergent social strata — from royal palaces to the worst slums — has shown me that the child obeys in his development natural laws which are identical for all."*

Most of Montessori's theories, which were original and controversial in the early twentieth century, have been accepted by today's child development specialists. Ironically, however, they have failed to touch many adults who have the actual care of young children. Hospital personnel still separate newborn babies from mothers and keep them in brightly-lighted nurseries, often noisy with cries from other infants. Toddlers are still confined for hours in playpens and high chairs which limit their natural impulse to explore. Well-meaning parents often lace a child's shoes for him long after he shows interest in doing it for himself. And many teachers still operate on the principle that the best learning occurs when children are sitting still and listening to an adult.

Unfortunately, much of Montessori's valuable advice remains obscure because of the style of her writing which does not attract the average reader. Many of Montessori's books are simply printed versions of her lectures which were transcribed from notes taken by her students. As such, they contain a great deal of repetition and vary in quality both in the original Italian and in the English translations. Nevertheless, each time that I read her books I find certain phrases and paragraphs of such pure wisdom that I want to share them with every other adult who has responsibility for a young child.

This volume represents my effort to do this. I have tried to highlight the insights of Maria Montessori which have been the most meaningful to me as a mother and teacher during the past twenty years.

Montessori's language may seem flowery and mystical in today's world but her intuition is amazingly sound and surprisingly applicable. She tells us repeatedly, *"If we want to help life, the first condition of success is that we shall know the laws which govern it."* These laws are continually revealed to the observant adult who pauses in his everyday life to really *"look at the child."*

Aline D. Wolf
Altoona, Pennsylvania
April 1978

The most important
   period of life
is not the age
   of university studies
but the period
   from birth to the age of six...
for that is the time
   when intelligence itself,
her greatest implement,
   is being formed....

At no other age

has the child greater need

of intelligent help....

In the first few days of life

the child must remain

as much as possible

in contact with the mother,

feeling the rhythm of her body

to which he is accustomed....

The tiny child's mind absorbs all his surroundings.... In his waking hours he should be with us to see what we do and hear what we say....

How closely the baby watches the
lips of a person speaking fondly
to her... gradually realizing that
the words are meant for her...
words which awaken that special
sensitivity which enables her to
absorb with ease an entire language....

Her mental

and physical development

are dependent on movement....

A child often cries

when he is confined

in a small space

which offers nothing

but frustration

to the exercise of his powers....

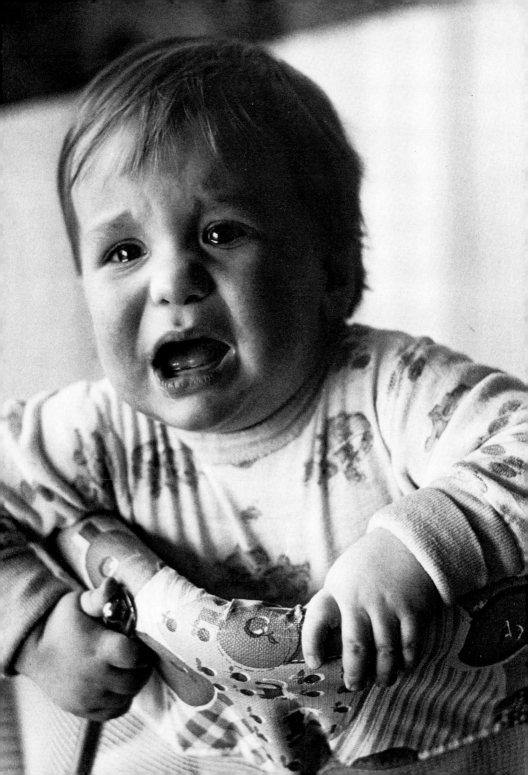

The child who wants to walk
by himself must be allowed
to try -- what strengthens
any developing power is
practice and repetition....

The child under two is well able to walk for a mile or so, and also to climb. Our impression that a long walk is beyond her comes from making her walk at our pace. But the child is not trying to "get there"-- all she wants is to walk. And because her legs are shorter than ours, it is we who must go at her pace....

Staircases

have the greatest appeal

because children

have in themselves

an innate tendency

to go upwards....

The child tends always

to expand her independence....

She wants to act of her own

accord, to handle things,

to dress and undress herself....

Her impulses are so energetic
that our usual reaction
is to check them.... But we
must consider that exploring
her environment is the child's
natural way of learning....

Her creative energies
are so fragile
as to need
a loving and
understanding response.

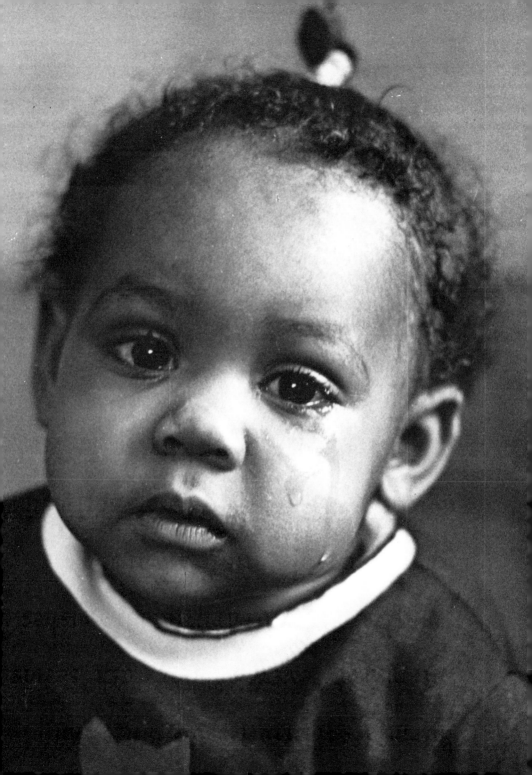

The young child passes through a series of sensitive periods during which he experiences an intense and specialized interest in the things around him ....

A particular object or a particular skill can awaken so much enthusiasm in him that it becomes incorporated in his very existence....

Little he cares

about the knowledge of others;

he wants to acquire

knowledge of his own...

to experience the world

through his own unaided efforts....

The senses,

being explorers of the world,

open the way to knowledge....

In order to learn
the child must first
be able to concentrate ....
But no one can force
concentration upon her.
She develops concentration
by fixing her attention
on some task she is performing
with her hands....

The hand

is the chief teacher

of the child ....

The first stretching out of the child's tiny hands should fill the observer with wonder and reverence. Instead the adult thinks only of protecting insignificant objects, constantly repeating, "Don't touch!"

The mind of the young child
is different from ours....
When we recognize the limitations
of reaching her
through verbal instruction,
then the whole concept
of education changes.
It becomes a matter of providing
an appropriate environment,
not forcing our words
upon her ears....

If the child is absorbed in a harmless activity we must not interrupt, even if her task seems pointless or contrary to our wishes. For the child must always be able to finish a cycle of activity on which her heart is set....

This kind of activity

which serves no external purpose

gives children

the practice they need

for coordinating their movements....

An adult works

   to perfect the environment...

A child works

   to perfect himself....

A child chooses

what helps him

to construct himself....

As he masters each new skill

his self-confidence increases....

Listening

    does not make a man...

Only practical work

    and experience

        lead the young

            to maturity....

Self-discipline begins
when she focuses
all her energy
on a useful exercise....

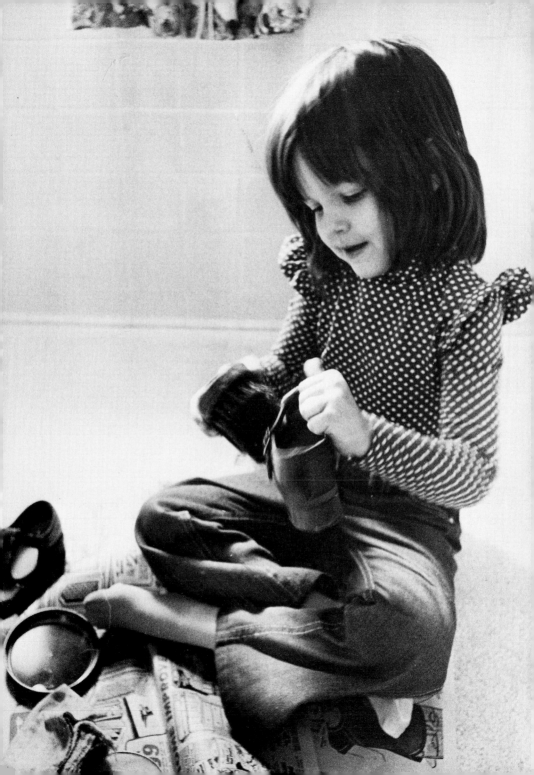

If we were to establish a primary principle, it would be to constantly allow the child's participation in our lives. For he cannot learn to act if he does not join in our actions, just as he cannot learn to speak if he does not hear....

To extend to the child this hospitality, to allow him to participate in our work, can be difficult, but it costs nothing. Our time is a far more precious gift than material objects....